BUTCHER & CO.

BUTCHER & CO.

Vincent O'Sullivan

Oxford University Press

Oxford London Glasgow
New York Toronto Melbourne Wellington
Ibadan Nairobi Dar Es Salaam Lusaka Cape Town
Kuala Lumpur Singapore Jakarta Hong Kong Tokyo

Published with the aid of the New Zealand Literary Fund

ISBN O 19 558023 O

Printed by The Caxton Press, Christchurch

Published by Oxford University Press,
Wellington

For Dunstan

ACKNOWLEDGEMENTS

Acknowledgements are due to the editors of the following publications, in which some of these poems have appeared: *Islands, Landfall, The Listener, Poetry New Zealand* (Pegasus Press, 1974).

CONTENTS

Of Places, Seasons

Of Butcher, Baldy, Related Matters

OF PLACES, SEASONS

RESTHAVEN

This morning we have opened
the Home for the Elderly
and Vogel Street did itself proud.

The Minister spoke
and the Rotarians applauded
and all in all it was pretty impressive.

The public stood at the bedroom doorways
approved of the deep-pile carpet
remarked on the comfy lounge and the widescreen telly.

It was beautiful Waikato morning
a top-dresser flew over the macrocarpa
the loudspeaker blared from the junior athletics

and the truth of yellow earth was never touched on.
The old woman with a silver-tipped cane
the man whose wife

must sleep in a different wing
smile shakily at us
their eyes crinkle against the sunlight,

say Thank you so much
for coming to see us off,
thank you for good wishes and applause

as they step inside
to the lobbyful of gladioli
and decorative fern,

where they keep smiling
at their families on the other side
like astronauts just before the countdown.

I touch an Indian figurine.
It is nothing like her, and yet
I have only her in mind.

She is in a city not my city
near a church I first heard of
as a child, in a song,

a church she sees from her door
and has never mentioned once
and when she is walking past it

her steps ring across its pavement.
I cannot claim for her extraordinary ease
with men or cities,

not say she is natural as bird
in the acacia nor oleander
under summer dust.

That kind of talk confuses.
There are only a few words *simple
direct sensuous complete*

and as they're said I doubt them.
I touch a figurine of crude iron,
no more unlike her than the words to say it.

PUKERORO—APRIL

At the farm our arrows shot
inaccurately but no less beautiful
above the old hawthorn over the ditch scraggy

as a row of women
their heads tangled together above a common tub,
our arrows red and blue and yellow

the black rings round the shafts
just in from the fletches you'd think were markings
on some bird once they're hissed and lifting

away there over the hawthorn
over the fences unfixed for ten, twelve years,
the wire sagged as in first war news-reels,

one of them falling next door
in the ragwort paddock
once the best herd here for miles

but the only son gone bad in Sydney,
abo women, gin, jesus you name it,
another lands back of the macrocarpa

its tail-feathers skewed on the way through
the yellow banged on the corrugated shed
nowhere near the tent torn out

to one flat canvas painted up to a smart
bull's-eye you'd spot from a top-dresser
a couple of miles off,

God knows there were so many shot
we didn't find didn't bother to look for
too hard either, and at night

when we've blamed each other for most of the losses,
the ten-acre level paddocks
the long high hedges

out there under pricking sky
ride tomorrow's frost,
and we're happy still from the childishness of it,

the mad Sherwood game
the children shouting *here comes Robin*
across dull mirroring water,

there's a bruise down your left arm
belted when wood first leaped still stinging–
and when you close your eyes the bird-like drift of it.

COMING BACK

We have come from a friend's coffin:
dark-grained, elaborately handled,
the inevitable ship
we have placed on the lip of earth
and stood by for a few minutes
and each of us thought
more perhaps of the endless polished sea
than our friend who is now a speck,
his voyaging already
as if further than merely minutes,
as though on a beach
we must turn now to each other,
ask who has a match,
watch that small flare like a signal
telling those near the shoreline
how passes are now cleared,
the weather certain,
we may straggle back over dunes,
the rattle of grasses,
the long curled drumming
a thinner and thinner line behind us,
and are touched by the curious boredom
as the old day opens,
the clack of car doors,
the upholstery mildly warm from the winter sun.

DROUGHT

Half a dozen words, in a season
when rain has held off for three months already,
when this morning we have put lime
on a rotting hedgehog that died of thirst.

There is no allegory in weather
            no symbol in the stretched skin
only *today* in the unexpected stench,
in the hills (as children say)
            like sleeping lions,
in the dust that rises if a cat pounce.

And half a dozen words.
We each hold them as a cup, water.
You have three which you hold to give.
I have three to give for them.

FOR A FRIEND COMING HOME

I shall tell you this
you may come back cradling
the old deception
our eel-shaped country slides in,
men equal as trees
before all weathers.

Yet know, friend, carrying that
you walk against rivers,
you must forget old songs
as you would a buried woman.
You must flake Christ from you
like a leper's crust.

FOR A THIRD BIRTHDAY

We sang 'happy birthday' three times over
we flicked the lights on then flicked them off
we clapped each time your small breath easily
called darkness in happy as a favourite cat.

Solemn as you like we wore paper hats
a white one for your aunt who makes brides' dresses
red ones for your cousins who sang and laughed
a blue one for your mother that matched her apron.

'Oh wasn't *that* a blow!' we call
and we shout across at each other and our words
stumble a bit at the wine and we catch at your laughing
because we are happy too and must laugh at something.

There's twenty minutes here while we don't care do we
much about the neighbours much about work
not at all about the names we're told to think of
when fun shakes the table—the hermit's skull

Freud and his special bag marked 'Family'
the horseman and his scythe patient at the doorstep
a countryman strident in his one refrain
how the Iron Mountain squats at the back of our laughter.

We want to ask them in, say 'be at home' don't we,
say 'stand back will you' while the three candles spitter
and there's dark around us all right but our ten voices tinker
with dark's paraphernalia. We say *wish*, we mean *here*.

THE WOMAN FROM THE HOME

The woman from the home
stood all day at the window

she loved the sky because it was open
she hated the earth because it was closed

the autumn was hands
the winter the flat of palms slapping on tables
the summer young hands still involved with winter.

All day she stood at the window
one wrist would touch like a stranger
her other wrist.

If she stood still
inside the window
looked long at the sky
then at times it happened–
she forgot she stood on carpet
she thought of trees like sisters.
'Growing out of' and 'growing into'
were sides of her tree.
But there was the sky always
and the sky shining as a brand-new bath.

She chose the river for death
because we cannot fly
and the earth must be left somehow
and the pure strain of the river
is a kind of heavy sky.
Not best or second best, but outside the window.

LONG DISTANCE

I take up my pen to answer,
my first words are at once a limitation,
my first phrase lays down

the track we shall follow, one of dozens
we might just as well have begun at,
choose a different word.

Yet nothing is made right through,
nothing completed.
Each word is a gamble on imperfection,

waits its taking up,
its acceptance, its giving semblance
of true arc homed to circle, taken as fact.

Our writing at all,
our holding pens between indecisive fingers,
facing inanities of space or paper,

is to sit it out through one season,
think and talk of two.
It is doubling as plough, snow-plough,

touching erratic purpose
through divagation,
arctic glitter in branches of a tropic palm.

Yet we go on with our telling
in half belief the story
consumes our need for fable;

half disbelief how appetite
transposes sense of fitness
to a mirror world.

TREASURE

There is a cabinet she likes people to look at,
postcards, cartridge cases, mouse-ear shells,
gum of various sizes—ugly transparent chips
like big toe-nails, bits as broad as fists,
one almost pale as cream where the bubbles
stand in a stiff row as you get in ice.
She'd heard that said forty, was it, years back?
And she'll say it now to those who look, 'like ice'
she'll say, who with all her life in the north
has never seen ice thicker than a skin on puddles.
                                    On the highest shelf,
the one eye-level with an average man,
there are adzes, flakes of obsidian, grooved
fishing weights, a perfect *mere*
museums have offered to buy, and alabaster
her brother lugged from Turkey after the war.
'And a shrunken head,' she'll tell you,
says her great-grandfather kept it in a special box,
he handed it on to her father's father
and somehow it was lost, though the box is here—
cracked foreign wood with a velvet lid.
So ice she'll talk of, and that Maori head,
lost between generations of canny farmers.
The cabinet, everything in it, those she talks to,
cloud for that half minute while she broods her loss—
the foot-thick ice from the south, the baked blue cheeks.

SLOW RIVER

The first day we might call real spring,
after late winter camellias
turned at their edges the way roses
behind Venus and her scalloped waves
browned with their weariness (remembering Pater).
The first day. Real spring.
Branches on the pendulous birches,
a week ago wires drooping
a kind of cage when you stood there
close to the trunk,
           today edged with a dozen
minute flares in each ten-inch span.

Myths by right should startle
the mind a quick second after eye's delighted
at the way rock has jittered,
the bandages unravelled, the hole
in a dead palm
           winked as the blood fires,
as sun's caught in streaming, carried.
Should be, then. Ought to.

The river slips down its black shelf
sun rides its varnished carriage like a blurred white
                       face.
The end of myths, the echoes . . .
'The final curiosity' that same author said
(his one fixed theme behind roses, venus),
riding the first day
           we might call *real spring*.
To touch sun's true earthly brilliance
take us deep,
         slow river.

NEIGHBOUR

With the same name as a famous athlete,
with a brother who went to the dogs in Aussie,
once the victim of a rape she now looks back on,
                    the local Cleopatra,
    the ancient joke,
                    waits at the stop near the Riverina.
She sucks at a dry fag
                    as a girl at a dream.
She eases the parcelled bottle in her white string bag.

The convent girls with breasts
                    like processional buds
eye her as they would a movie from another decade,
a prophecy too absurd for a nun to gloss.
The bus driver with his dog-eared *Sexus*
the teacher with his hair in a band
                    (his secret wish to star as Hamlet)
the Czech from the bottlestore who has seen far worse
circle her as tourists
                    an Egyptian corpse.
She lives in hieroglyphics, behind fingered glass.
        Yet she'll ride the bus beside them
like the painted barge.
                    There is no wind she'll acknowledge
flutters time like petals,
none at her puckered face as a brush on bone.

When she stands with her string bag
                    to pull at the cord
when her lurch almost humps her
                    on the driver's back
the girls choke on their hat brims,
                    even Hamlet smiles.
She floats the bus's aisle like that true dark river.
Her rickety queenship quells them, the local raver.
On the naked road she's a smear between dust and evening.

The doors hush behind her like palace sluts.

22

ALMOST STILL LIFE

After an afternoon spent reading
a poet who loved death like his own reflection
(and he loved that all right, in a hundred verses)
the town seems duller than before I walked
past alkies, lovers, in their special garden,
their stone maze at the side of the library,
up the steps to the long bright room
where stacked assistants lift my eyes from reading,
indifferent (if looking back's a sign to go on)
these ladies in their black stockings
as God told of a plague, or floods, or churches
tilted by sagging piles until the divine eye
sags too in a tall mosaic, quite shut from the ground.
'The southerly's abated' says one girl
near a window, the clouds hang on her words
like grey streaked rags.
                    The other, with calves
long as a syllabus for legal practice
cradles a bored bust where she leans and glances
over her magazines, the topmost cover
vaguely chinese from here, its stiff green figures,
Noël, Noël, voici nos rois mages
the thick snake of text between tit and art.

KAKA

We didn't even know him from a book
when a bit of the sky flapped red and 'Look!'

we called to each other and felt blood rush
that something so unexpected from time and bush

had dropped towards us then swooped again
to the top of the paulonia while a gauze-like rain

so light it rested beads on our sleeves and hair
touched us as it touched him swaying there

while under he arced and tapped at the dry husks,
making a game of wheels between jab and rasp.

We watch for him now each day but can't *expect*
a thing so stained with freedom to elect

that it's here his wings will cover a quiet street
with a colour we hadn't thought so likely to meet

by looking up one morning just after eight.
He's like dark and furling smoke and a touch of fate.
He brings to the early day what we thought was late.

ONLY NATURAL THINGS

Here are garden things she loved,
For her eyes we look
At wisteria in her birthday's month
That falls across pine and back
Towards the house and the shaded room
Where I and my children take

Not a sprig of that blue flare
For our grieving's badge,
Not a branch where it leans on the pine
Or at the path's rough edge,
But the lift of the sky it seems, from here,
The crammed sky, as pledge.

There is no day among September days
Not that vine's natural
Stage between scarcely hinted
And immeasurably full,
Hail at month's far beginning,
At month's end, *Farewell.*

AUCKLAND DOMAIN

A dozen people at least ten of them English
sit round their thermos and their boiled eggs
as a tribe circling its totem, they have camped here
under warm autumn sun, beneath foreign trees.
In a circle of oaks further down the slope
Tongans spread colour like a new sea.
This could be a dream for the half hour I sit here,
better than a dream, I bite my cheek, I feel it,
children fall laughing they get up crying,
there are arms for each, there is calling that raises
a couple of score pigeons, their odd wet clapping.
And beside a maple, near giant magnolias compacted
like—so one tells the children—elephants shoving,
a scrap of *fin-de-siècle* at the top of the hill,
marble and metal and the bite of weather—
an eighteen-inch Valkyrie, her sickle-horn,
green stippling her arm while she gathers breath.

FUNCTION

I slice bread after a morning's drinking,
eating, after words substantial as meringues,
conversations waxy as paper cups.
Writers have quoted themselves on the front steps,
the hosts stood near their fish-pond
where fins sank like coins, lilies flapped fatly.
Culture's Santa who reined down from the north
declared his snappy jacket, his suede jaws,
his presence undoubted as a boil's.
                      Six hours later (now) with clouds
marching across the hills of the lead-dull harbour
I speak with a half-pissed doctor of China,
of wars we didn't see, of heaped statistics.
He says how progress (i.e. not so much pain, less work, less anger)
would take the shine from that fat rubbed apple
we writers need for our world, *our human range.*
We sit (still holding glasses) solemn as cats.
              Stuffed, sodden, certain
in our ringed-in city where ideas turn
slowly as ancient fish, as twenty years ago, or thirty . . .
The edge of the knife runs last light from the harbour.
Bread under my hand could be a stone.

LAST THINGS

She is planning her movement from him
more delicately than an old lady
runs the thread along her tongue
or holds up to the light the small silver noose,
says *ah!* and the needle's ready.
                She is careful in this
as our tact with tomorrow's dead
in saying 'Home again soon, are we?',
keeping the fresh handkerchief like a bullet
in one's sleeve, along one's wrist,
through the unbelieved,
                the unbelieving lie.
She prepares his breaking
with the slow skilful patience of sewing,
death.
        As carefully, he lets her,
knows how his ceasing breath takes half of hers,
that without cloth to work on, her own flesh must prick.

AT HOME IN ARGOS

In a house where two cats occasionally scuttle,
she opens her drawer as though committing secrets,
takes letters tied with pink librarian's tape,
hears cellophane crackle on photographs she looks at
once in four, five months.
                She holds several small diaries
which press the neat lines of her careful script,
the lovers she recorded as things to remember.
She reads a date, a place, a word she cannot decipher
without better light.
                She is Helen,
who once had a town to read by.

WARD TEN

There was always a girl with him.
As he grew older, so grew the girls younger,
his fine handsome greyness
                against faces like orchards
if you think of them in springtime,
the delicacy, the colour, the lack of substance.
And at a certain point he stopped ageing,
or so it seemed, and paradoxically the flesh
habitually at his side was gradually older,
twenty-eight then forty,
                the bronzed limbs paler,
the hair touched now and then with his own greyness,
until holding the matron's hand who was never married
he said over and over
a girl's name heard when he was twelve,
a girl called to by her father
on the inter-island ferry,
                a few miles out from the Heads,
and then never seen.
                Between beds white as lifeboats
the deck heaves again.

OWNING UP

By holding a cracked mirror
in front of the face

by turning it so that light
lays across it perfect

for giving back what the face
reflects to put there

one observes how the beautiful
glance aside, relieved,

the ugly pore for minutes
at the helpful suture,

the crazy are joined
by the black jagged rainbow.

And after mirror-talk
and the talk of sun's slanting,

honest gazing,
dry speculative reading,

one touches one's own face
which is touching

from hair-line to chin
the grating slip of edges.

AT YEATS'S GRAVE

A day of pilgrimage, but scarcely grace.
Lissadel and Rathcar, the road to Rosses Point—
and an hour's drive to the north, a boy's face
takes the smash of a bomb.
                                    The day grows faint
as I stand by the famous stone among winter trees,
the country blurred with cloud. A mile back
the TV news brings intellect to its knees,
the boy's eyes carved to identical rock.

We indulge the white page with its vivid ink,
remembering those rhymes for edging blood
to enterprise or fineness, watch Cuchulain think
his demon killed by rage in each new flood.
There is no eye to cast, and unseated horsemen.
The 'indomitable Irishry' refuse again.

Drumcliff, April '75

MELANCHOLY DRINKERS: SLIGO

The first people in the West arrived for the funeral,
they have been ready for the wake for a thousand years.
A nation that sits at the edge of its own mind,
watches the sun slide between headland and sea
like candles in the hands of mourners
sliding on polished wood the doubleness of flame.
Coming back I taste like drink that melancholy,
know I am not too late for obsequies.
'You've brought good weather with you', and I think
if the crucifix when they turn snips in the sun,
or the serge of the bereaved shows its shiny patches,
then I might as well answer 'Yes, I suppose I have.'
My fellow mourners push a pint towards me,
we lean at the window, watch the cloud cover
the long flat mountain laid out before us.
The day tips into dark as we knew it would.

ANOTHER WAY

There is another way of talking
which none of us care to give ear to.
It is putting one's hand straight in the knife drawer
then taking it out, transformed.

It is saying without 'like' or 'perhaps'
or 'remember' or 'do you think . . .'
that this was a room lived in for ten years
and now it is empty, and the door closed.

It is walking down the yard
beneath the trees that are thin as pencils
and a few months later loaded with summer
and saying, yes, one tree among seasons.

There is also listening to that talking
which is not eyes on the distance
and not fingers drumming beside the teapot
but listening as a shore might when tide rises.

It is time then to step from the verandah,
shut the children's gate at the top step,
take the few feet that spaces
where I am for a lifetime from where, now, I was.

And once that is done, the drawer closed,
the trees left to their turning,
the room with only the fluffy tacks from the carpet,
the road stands clean as a mirror. Our fingers heal.

APRÈS NOUS

Once the last gap in the hedge has grown over,
the foot's smear along grasses returned to blank smoothness,
the stoat at home in the hut where the lovers lay,

then paradise, indeed, is something to sing of:
it is the child's clap at the band rounding a corner,
the alkie's eye wheeled across the label

on a bottle he finds unemptied in a public toilet,
a note from the bank regretting an earlier note.
It is picking up a chunk of weathered marble

near an excavation for new apartments
and touching the thick curl of a fraction
of a small acanthus leaf from the top of a column,

the heart jumping, *Rome!* The river
slips for a moment between more dazzling banks,
the sacred candlestick in the centuries' mud and shit

noses very faintly, like a squad of eels.
All is back, back.
                    The black veil flaps white

in the shining wind, the old man
is a young man watching an ancient woman's hair
blaze out in sunset.

              Or in dark, sad Adam,
there is ploughing recalcitrant fields, finding slur of water,
by the covering cherub's incandescent thumb.

BACK WHERE WE STARTED

I was going to cut the macrocarpa
   and make a fence.
I talked about it to friends,
   worked out the expense
to plant acacias and birches
   until *almost* dense
they'd beautifully cut the late sun
   from quite blinding sense.

Then I learned the chopped boles
   before long would rot
and the plan for a rustic fence
   from the stumps was not
likely to get from my head
   to an actual plot.
Scant sun and the old tangle
   is what we've got.

OF BUTCHER, BALDY, RELATED MATTERS

BUTCHER IN SUNLIGHT

Butcher in sunlight picking at teeth with a comb-end
his eyelids half over his eyes
his left hand in his trouser pocket idling

gives late Friday a belch
from lung to lip *ah lovely!*
faces evening lean as a good carcase.

O Butcher how Friday latesun falls
touching the tip of your shoes with minute lighthouses
fetches bright stubble beneath your jawline.

For Sheila out the back still dredging beauty
from compact tube phial you're the very man
she could take you in slices like bacon

and no beg pardons. Butcher, her eyes grace you
gross there in sunlight. *You're miracle, man.*

BUTCHER TALKS ON TIME

'Well' Butcher says 'they're all in for an end
the old stuff with its tall columns
the middle stuff with its pointy arches
the jumble of all the others
stations palaces airports racetracks.
That's the only vision *I* know.
Dust to dust.'
          His cleaver glints
up and down through the ribs. He breaks
the cage, there's nothing to fly out.
(A small blob of kidney in the sawdust
could though be canary's head, gone ruffly.)
Time's the sweat under his armpit
Sheila's quick grunt (lovely!)
it's the thin needle white as God
knocking the figures back
when your foot's right down.

'Well' says B. again 'we're all in for an end.'

KNUCKLE

Knuckle on bone like
    knee in plushy groin
reeks exhilaration
    a warm cord
from hairy mit
    from cave's mutter
threads pretty neatly
    shines right through
you're a bead man
    you're glassy
and you're in there Butcher
    fisting away
when *ah* sweet spurting
    like God say riding home
bone barks back
    target shimmers

WAYS OF TELLING A SOLDIER

'Not feathers that make the bird as they say
there's ways of telling a soldier naked as sky'
                    B. argues one day with a digger
'Bullets'll stud you a neat tunic four neat mean bullets
    that's how you tell a soldier dig
                that cuts a military figure.'

BUTCHER SPEAKS CRUDELY OF
BREAKING IT OFF

As far as Butcher goes
   you can truncate love
any bleeding day of the week
   with or without a glove

to give your knife work
   class and tone
it comes to the same thing
   says Butcher
all comes to the same thing
   that's flash and groan.

eh Butcher?

B.'s NIGHTMARE

In nightmare having for once
cut things too fine
seeing his hand five red noughts
unfingered Butcher
raises his hand like a sky
five streaming comets
says Well I shall be a singer
and when his throat
clogs like a jammed oyster
says Feet will save me
till a train takes his good idea
clean as a whistle
merely two bleary tunnels
where Butcher ends
Then he jokes looking down
no legs to speak of
I shall pose as roasts
on TV commercials
but wakes again unwealthy
legs poor beneath him.

SENTIMENTAL

Morning after an epic B. likes
(knife *whishing* at stone)
to think about almost casual
something very lovely
like when the Roman legions
crossed the crest of a blue hill
then down a curving road
that dipped and rose up
and supposing anyone noticed
from an opposite hill
where the Roman army hung
then he'd see flashed at him
in imperial sunlight
half that bloody hillside
crammed with all those helmets
like ten thousand teeth.

Odd
  I have never noticed
  man operating without God
  acts so very better
  than the true believer
said a man who came into
the shop's
cool, something of a raver,
Butcher thought, between chops.

What do you mean?
B. asked
  what does all that mean?

Give me your knife's what I mean.

That'd be giving God up all right, B. said.

Exactly, the man said,
  you make the team.

POWER STICKS SAYS B. AS
THE FAN FLINGS

The old story of the apple
is balanced on every nipple
I've seen B. confesses
the same old stain
from clot-fingered Cain,
that depresses
even me, *Butcher,*
but Power's the bit that will get me
that's where the rot began
that pressed the first button for the last forget-me
that's nearly the end of the song if you'll let me
that (he refrains) *is when rot began*
that is picking the bones of the last man, man.
'Oh Power,' says Butcher, 'that's when
that's when the shit *really* hits the fan.'

B.'s THOUGHTS ON NATURE

He'd go a long way to see a whale, B. would.

Imagine those ribs to begin with
a cathedral you could walk down
over the tongue like a doormat to begin with
then down you'd walk side-chapels
bigbone pillars one gutsy vault
you could fit a choir in there,
sing the National Anthem solid
while the great tail wrapped round the sky
the sweetest flag you'd seen you'd nearly cry
it'd be so mighty.
                         Or likewise imagine
riding if you could its glassy back
the meanest little eye all you could see
like a bloody mouse it'd seem steering a rocket.
The splash you'd make then, Butcher!
She'd slap down easy for fathoms
turn wrecks if she wanted like a kid
turning then throwing cards across a carpet
only some carpet too, bits of gold if you like
twenty-ton anchors cannons about right
for a quick flick.
                         That'd be something
make them sit up brother, a Town Hall
made of meat flying your apron
saying *Welcome Aboard Earthling* or
Here's Nature—Ride It.

The things you could do with a whale, Butcher!

BUTCHER ON LIFE IN GENERAL

Do not despair
   says Butcher seeing flesh drop
from an old relative as surely
    as luncheon say from the slicer
      in the shop
Do not despair
   says Butcher when talk of God
and how He's gone for good
    makes B. yawn and nod
Do not despair
   he comforts young jane preggers
he tells the senior citizen with his lean
Do not despair
   we're tucked safe down here forever
the winds at the end of the world will blow us clean.

SINKING IT

Do I feel great! she mutters musky
a matter of earthly minutes
         after galaxies shifted slightly
for *Man, could he feed it!*
           oh amazonian Sheila
her silksac breasts still fog about him
       Great! she says again
and Butcher remarking nothing
            merely feels the runnels
carve down from his armpits
his hair stuck to his scalp itchy with strain
for *Honeyworld of Women,*
          be in on this:
when the Butcher's heart isn't in it
         then it's digging ditches,
even lifting the right word's
          fairly hefty yacker
though he crams his eyes on moonlight,
thinks of starmuff solid.
So now when she *has* to talk
           it's rubbing salt.
Gee Butcher she says at a stretch
       I feel titanic!
And B., mean as a current,
          Call me iceberg.

BUTCHER'S FAVOURITE STORY

A woman was walking along the road wheeling a pram when she passed beneath a window, where a man balanced a box of used car-parts upon a two-inch ledge. The man leaned forward to get a better view of the woman, and the box fell and crushed the baby's head. Naturally the woman was angry and insisted that he give her the box of spare parts, in exchange for the baby whose head was flattened like a plate with a face painted on it. The man felt guilty (especially as he knew that he had leaned forward to observe the young mother's breasts) and agreed to the exchange. The mother covered the box with a shawl and continued down the road. The man, however, was at a loss until he smiled to himself, went back to his room on the second floor, and balanced the baby on the window-sill, waiting for another woman with attractive breasts to wheel past a pramful of used car-parts.

AN EASY ALLEGORY ON MIND/BODY AND THE
SWEETNESS OF PERSONAL ART

Butcher's cousin Baldy whom you'll hear of
carries about in his head a pocket mirror
or vice versa
        which means pretty thinking
about himself *always*
      or suppose disaster comes
like a swift kick or a sudden
          sitting down
the splinters are part of himself
         the thin bleeps
of tragedy then siphon through the ether
his mind his bum good buddies
thank his portable mirror

rolling his eyes back whitish
       to see the inside mirror
feeling his pants pocket
       where's that silver sliver
You shall never know
      he tells Butcher
what true art means
      ho-hum B. thinks
grizzles a mean knife along the stone
switches fat from liver
     hears blood tick like a watch
on his marvellous shoes.

ADVICE AS B.C. (FOR BALDY CRITICUS) COMPOSES

Baldy sits at a cleared desk when B. comes in.
Baldy looks up looks down points without looking
to chair where B. may/
              to couch on which he does
take ease.
         Baldy chips at fine-grained
nature, says 'Making a poem.'
'Like this,' he tells, carving small block bees.
They already sprinkle his blotter
              like a smashed-in hive.
'You observe' he condescends 'how my bees
take form, the wings we both may see through
              as good as whirring.'
And 'Those blackish-yellow colours like for real,
I've put there.'
              With you so far, Baldy.
But Butcher puzzles.
            Baldy bends low,
pinkcheeks at them, huffing,
swings his arms as if bees'll copy,
thrashes air till sweat specks beady
            high balding brow.
The yellow-black neatwingers dead as stones.

'Where brother,'—so Baldy as poet muddles
            —'do we go now?'
Think of flies Butcher tells him *stuff the bees.*
There's a dirty smear on the blotter.
            Baldy grieves.
Corrupt the words! B. shouts him. *Compose yourself!*

There's a buzz in the room even surprises Butcher.

MUST BE AGEING

A girl a few days out from high school
  about three weeks before her first seduction
due January the First four hundred hours
  on the sunrise side of the Mount
that girl her legs in tight denims
  her bottom which is not yet arse
delicate oh delicate as a praying mantis
  her hair like frozen wind
you look at her B. walk in you remember
  first time you saw the sea as a child
the first time snow ticked down
  with that frying noise on the car-roof
when your father parked for a snort at Waiouru
  you're looking at spokes of sunlight
the stones in a pool picked bright as money . . .
  This is pure sentiment, Butcher!
  Give the girl her chops.

STILL SHINES WHEN YOU THINK OF IT

Stood on the top of a spur once
the grunt before Sheila sharp beside him
a river shining like wire ten miles off
the sky clean as a dentist's mouth
jesus *Was* it lovely!
        and the hills folded and folded
again and the white sky in the west
still part of the earth
        there's not many days like that eh
when your own hand feels a kind of godsweat
fresh on things like they're just uncovered.

And not fifty feet from the spur
a hawk lifted
        and for two turns turned like one wing
was tacked to the air
        and then she's away
beak a glint as she's turning
so the grunt sighs like in church
and even Butcher
        yes Butcher too
thinks *hawkarc curries the eye all right*
gives your blood that push
while the mind corrupts as usual
with 'proportion' 'accuracy' etcetera
those stones we lift with our tongues trying to say
        ah! feathered guts!
And she's closing sweet on something,
death, that perfect hinge.

It still shines when you think of it,
        like that river.

PENTECOST

'What was over their heads
           was twelve pocket transistors
celestial stations beaming
bits of electronic heaven gleaming
and the great DJ
spieling out his pretty
           as Jesus with rose-
red lipsticky palms
           line on love, eh Sheila?
Talk about resurrection—
how those long-hairs dug it!
—except Thomas that is
who still believed Marconi
was a made-up dago
     and Adam deaf from that cross
crammed for a heavy weekend
           in his bony ear.'

It wasn't like that sobs Sheila
and Butcher lighting
     a match in the early evening
for once feels pity tickle
says *I know that honey.*
           See! he says
his fingers cupped like wings
     and the flame there, riding.

HOLD IT

There's a high sweet figure
   inside every butcher

casually bent in his saddle
   lighting up against the wind

his hands cupping a match
   like a yellow stone.

He sits eyes grave as a camera
   his horse carved beneath him.

It's high up, he's sitting,
   the sky behind him, blazing.

Far off the river turns
   like a glass-backed lizard

the hills reach high in the blue
   where a few hawks stud it.

Butcher with luck will cross him
   say one dream in a dozen.

They gaze each other cool.
   Suck the same butt, sweetly.

DO YOU EVER CONSIDER

In a former life Butcher may have been
so beautifully cut that Olympic athletes
hurried their clothes back on before they were seen
by *those* empyrean eyes,
                    in front of *those* limbs.
He may have been so priestly faced
a whore couldn't have seen him without shedding hymns.

And there's nothing a man on a dull winter morning
absently over the parsley he arranges neatly
can't have done in the line of brawling, of exotic spawning.

Where you see a striped apron there may hulk a hero
in two shoes the eleven feet of Capone and Spartacus, Don Juan
                    and Captain Ahab, M. J. Savage, Nero.
Between blade and block there may lie the head of Pharoah.

Here may be the horn
                to outhorn Roncevalles
the boot to fill Eden Park
a heart so chocker with love for all things born
it shines self-contained as the host in a church's dark.
And his possible animal faces may fill the Ark.

  Lips of lords and ladies
  wait for the hands that sprinkle parsley.

THAT'S US

A country Baldy complains where all ambition
pares down so that his and my condition
stand level-headed, identically shod.
'That's what comes' Baldy will tell you
                    'when equality's your God.'

Bring back the whip if you will advises Butcher
Merit's a queen until you catch her
then naked-limbed and her breasts full
you'll find when you clamber on her
                    your lips push dirt from a skull.

'That simply invokes the end of every dream.'

It's the only ground we stand on while the minutes cram.

IT FOLLOWS THEN

If I sit here and whittle
  a man from a skewer
dream for a bit as I do
  of that distant rider
I have put it off for an hour
        at least, or a half

if I chisel a new grunt
  next week up the Coast
should I nick the side of my thumb
  like a just-pushed peach
I have put it off for a minute
        or even more

and there's this thought, Baldy,
  it's clear as the morning
if the Rider blew in my eyes
  his ice-blue circles
if another glint talked quicker
  than my precious own
I have put it off forever.
        Take my point?

THE HUMAN CONDITION, SHALL WE SAY?

No way B. says
    for Baldy's just told him
    spilled those famous words
Rousseau he's intoned for example *The Noble Savage*
strung out *Pacific Paradise, Human Rights,*
Space and *Dignity* and . . .
like he was singing the field at an Auckland Cup.

Yet *Hell!* B. tells him
    you shift your fences Baldy
    but that's not space.

Then B. does an odd thing
leans right across Baldy's desk
grabs his globe of the world
gives that globe a spin
(the colours pink into blue one whirring stream)
then says
    his finger dropping smartly
Right, you've a gutsful, cobber?
You want to take it elsewhere where the air's a dream?

Over the rushing world
          one finger falls
stops the rush with a nail and Butcher calls
    Don't tell me I'm changed Baldy,
        just because I'm Here!
Then a straight-as-kauri Delphi from an island shore:
    simply by railing with a new inflection
        your engorgement's whirled.

A GOOD JOKER'S HOMER

Loved it when he read it
browsing (so Baldy thought) and kind of cowlike
that cultured paddock
        those talklong Baldy shelves
where Butcher just picked one
    sat there solemn
opened it like a grave you might as well say
when out jumped small as life
    coolgloss Ulysses
    Achilles the All Black skipper
with his taste for scrums
chattering Cassandra (could be Sheila's mum)
dream-laden Helen we close our fists on
    even sad outsmarted Ajax
hacked off as the Works' foreman
              at a secret ballot.
Well who'd have thought
          B. admits
there's good stuff here.
          Likes to think most and most
for days weeks after
    of queen of pig island
         of pylon-tall Circe
a batch at Taupo swinging one starry boob
a two-tone convertible purrs from the other.
Radio Hauraki pipes from old Swine Grotto.

There's another bit that gets me
    and *Oh?* says Baldy.
Not as you might expect the grubby pages
Zeus getting his greens regular as swanwork
the poncy boys caught out at the post-game party
Thersites chalking his words on the grandstand wall
    no not these at all
It's this
    says the quiet Butcher
It's the piece about what comes after.
        About twittering ghosts.

FÊTED

It had to happen.
      B. & B., kinsfolk, brokers,
on the same moon, target,
for identical fodder, famish–
            ah Girl
(*grunt-goddess* should minds work a merger)
raises her pale disc above man and man.
Books flake like a white disease tells Baldy's Cressid,
Knives, oh their dull stunts she unbuckles Butcher.
Paper and metal,
          serpent and dove, *she's got 'em.*
B. will stand listless before stacked ages
B. will gloom distant above chopped minutes
man into wolf and back as moon dictates them,
or cage you might say one minute, prairies next.

'You cannot lay your thumb in a book' frets Baldy
'reel your gazing out above land and water,
do that, keep career shiny, hold fame erect?'
'Not *fame* that's certain'
          says the Butcher vilely
but there's no heart in his dirt-talk
          no dirt in his heart.
Imagine that block spring lilies–
          What's so odd? he queries.
Miracle (*sb*.L., OF., *object of wonder*)
flares them naked as moon
          over seas converging.
Slides along cousin muzzles.
          4 sly/purest eyes.

YOU KNOW SOMETIMES BALDY HOW HE GETS ME

You know sometimes Baldy how he gets me
his talk a neater skewer than I'll concede

says how can you talk of sincere say
when your very skill weighs death in ounces

says how without smirking work breasts erotic
as though you'd not heard of slicer, not heard of honing?

I do not believe says Baldy you can live through spring.
You do not find a camellia in the guts of a pig.

And anger'll wash me then like a sudden hose,
its bright grainy streaming in front of my eyes.

A second may spread like a decade that's lived out *butcher,*
one pulse fit all the dates which *you* know, Baldy.

And it's odd this, when that stream is clearing,
when road as much as bird or man as sky comes scoured,

and I open my eyes slowly as though daylight stings—
the Rider's eyes match mine like a mirror.

Innocent as meat.

SING OR TALK IT, SINGING

Come, here's a Butcher's piece
you wouldn't have hoped
to hear while my sweet feet tinkered
to avoid trade slopped
but my mind's eye shines to itself
with how Helen raped
sang in her turn *Love's fancy walking*
beside the narrow river couldn't touch this for loving.

In another piece between fridge
and the combed sawdust
yellow as handled hair
I sing *Oh for that past*
which tells *tomorrow's ever*
lined up like coast
as the Rider might see it, get me, no beginning, end,
as his eye hooked to horizon makes the straight coast bend.

And singing a word remarks it
that'll go without saying
I sing *Butcher* before my queues
the word outstrops my braying
each world is made in a breath
while its shape waits, tiring.
Oh speech'll turn like Pharos in an old bald book.
Sing! it'll crave at eye's end, on tongue's tip, *look!*

WAKING INTO IS IT, OR THE OTHER WAY?

It may be at this or at that end of a tunnel
it may be you I shall face in a moment
                    it may be you face me.
There is a whirr like the turn of a fan
                    at the back of morning.
Oh I/you say
                    here is rise from ether
here is labyrinth unthreaded
                    the slowing of the fan to one blade
                                        in sunlight.
Either way or all see how dawn moves edgy
along the high hills across windowsills beside us
                    catch how blood tips in your ear
at the first bird's chitter
at step's clip on the pavement
            at the first match striking.
Baldy stirs so does Rider so do I/friend/you.
The mates front up for a fresh one.
                    Here comes the Butcher.